CONSERVATORY
GARFIELD PARK

LONDON. CRYSTAL PALACE.

THE JEWEL BOX, FOREST PARK, ST. LOUIS, MO.—3

Greenhouse, Hudson River State Hospital.

Poughkeepsie, N. Y.

CHATSWORTH—THE GRAND CONSERVATORY

Conservatory at Rose Gardens, Druid Hill Park, Baltimore, Md.

3A-H196

EDEN PARK CONSERVATORY, CINCINNATI, OHIO

5A-H250

4064X. Greenhouse,
S. O. Home, Normal, Ill.

37 - Conservatory, Golden Gate Park, San Francisco.

THE ROSE PERGOLA, KEW GARDENS.

The Grand Plaza. Canadian National Exhibition, Toronto.

Palmhouse. Sefton Park. LIVERPOOL.

Conservatory in Wright Park,
Tacoma, U. S. A.

G.11   HAMPTON COURT PALACE   *H. M. Office of Works*
THE GREAT VINE

52. - RENNES. - Les Serres du Jardin des Plantes

Collection A. G.

WIEN, Schloß Schönbrunn, Palmenhaus   45753

PALM HOUSE, KEW GARDENS.

CONSERVATORY GARFIELD PARK, CHICAGO, ILL.   1672

MR. PAUL DE LONGPRE - CORNER IN HIS GARDEN
HOLLYWOOD, CALIFORNIA

SUNKEN GARDEN AND CONSERVATORY IN MITCHELL PARK, MILWAUKEE, WIS.

The Plant House, Mount Holyoke College, South Hadley, Mass.

THE CONSERVATORY, EMPRESS HOTEL,
VICTORIA, B.C., CANADA

for Mom

GARDENS & GLASS

GARFIELD PARK

CONSERVATORY

The Earthly Delights of the Garden of Glass   Barbara Rose

The greatest living master of the ancient medium of glass, Dale Chihuly has breathed new life into a traditional art form, ensuring its future by creating a third-millennium fine-art expression for an artisanal form invented before the first millennium began. This is a unique accomplishment, which is the result of the unusual mix of talents, risk taking, experimentation, organization, and social interaction that characterizes this visionary artist. Chihuly has the perceptive blend of precision and nonchalance, control and nerve, not only to find new solutions, but also to conceptualize new problems. His obsession with technical innovation, together with a healthy respect for the achievement of past masters, permits him to make a singular contribution to his chosen medium.

Chihuly has single-handedly elevated glass from craft to art. At the same time, he has reconciled glassblowing with the demands of contemporary avant-garde concerns and aesthetics. Emphasizing the inherent characteristics of solid yet transparent glass, he extends its capacity to transmit and reflect vibrant color. Chihuly has observed, and remains true to the fact, that glass is one of the few materials that transmit light and radiate color. Constantly experimenting with the properties and potential of his material, he has developed an extended and novel palette with a broad range and complexity at precisely the moment that color

field painting seems to be in decline. His daring permits him to achieve stunning visual effects—indeed, the very optical effects to which recent abstract painting aspires, but which its physical characteristics fail to deliver. The inescapable conclusion is that the transparent, delicate, watercolor-like effects that staining color into canvas achieved, Chihuly delivers in a more immediate and powerful way in glass.

There is a degree of subversion, one must admit, if not perversity, in this unprecedented metamorphosis of glass from handheld, small-scale, liquid-bearing vessels to immense architectural installations of extravagant proportions so enormous we may actually enter them. Mies van der Rohe may have conceived of the glass house as a minimalist transparent box, but there is something intrinsically absurd and fantastic in Chihuly's idea of glass towers, temples, and bridges that reminds one of the architectural extravaganzas of Ludwig, the mad, imaginative king of Bavaria.

Chihuly actively seeks new challenges to stimulate his creativity and imagination. During the 1970s, he first experimented with installations incorporating plate glass, along with ice and neon, in outdoor settings. Much later, again wanting to use glass out-of-doors, as part of nature, he designed a project centered on a river and involving artificial nature, with glass forms hanging from trees or floating in water. Recently he extended the artificial-paradise metaphor to its fullest development in the Garfield Park Conservatory installation in Chicago. Designing this installation was yet another opportunity to push his own limits and those of his medium. One suspects that the great irony of putting a glass garden inside a glass house must also have appealed to his contrarian sense of the bizarre and whimsical.

Chicago's Garfield Park Conservatory, a two-acre-long, glassed-in tropical garden, is one of the largest conservatories in the United States. In November 2001, Chihuly created more than thirty glass installations dispersed among the exotic plants, entwined in their branches and trunks, suspended in space, or floating in artificial ponds. Scattered throughout the hothouse, they were identified as *Peacock Blue Tower*, *Persian Pond*, *Macchia Forest*, *Basket Forest*, *End-of-the-Day Palm Tree*, *Fern Room Niijima Floats*, *Black Saguaros*, *Desert House Red Reeds*, *Ikebana*, *Venetians*, *Putti*, *Tiger Lilies*, and *Tree Urchins*. Most installations contain elements first used in other contexts, but now recontextualized in a site-specific assemblage installation. Glass reeds, fronds, vines, blossoms, bouquets, garlands, a fanciful Art Nouveau Tiffany-type snake, and a whimsical mock Renaissance garden fountain of a toadstool sitting on a turtle topped by a gold glass putto are interspersed with the living botanical displays. The contrast between natural and artificial nature elicits a sense of wonderment and marvel that makes the familiar setting seem altogether new.

Because Chicago is a city Chihuly has always liked, the Garfield Park Conservatory site was particularly appealing. He was especially intrigued by the project because there is water in nearly every room, and he finds subtle ways to interact with it. The variety, profusion, and color of Chihuly's vitreous blossoms, pods, and stalks contrast effectively with those of the myriad natural specimens in the botanical garden gathered from tropical climates for transplantation to the Windy City. Chihuly's creations, however, are products not of nature but of the human imagination.

They strike such a resonant chord that we may even imagine a Jungian interpretation. In their spiky protuberances, intense colors, and Medusa-like tentacles, they remind us on the one hand of the surrealistic floral paintings of Joseph Stella, and on the other of the zoomorphic filigrees filling the pages of medieval manuscript illumination as marginalia, and they are products of deep levels of consciousness.

The combination of seduction and glamour at the edge of repulsion has a powerful appeal for a contemporary sensibility formed by the images of science-fiction imagery. Are Chihuly's offbeat humor and quirky view of reality perhaps the product of a zeitgeist that has also produced the perverse subversion of glamour typical of the films of director David Lynch? For example, in the opening scene of Lynch's classic *Blue Velvet*, the colors of a lawn are surrealistically intensified and strange vegetation suddenly sprouts and expands out of control. Hybrids grow into menacing monsters.

The other image of a supernatural garden that comes to mind is centuries away from Lynch but rather the product of a genuinely Gothic imagination. In the late fifteenth century, Flemish artist Hieronymous Bosch painted the bizarre, unforgettable *Garden of Earthly Delights*, a hellish picture of the tortures of the damned that is the opposite of the earthly paradise of the Garden of Eden. Bosch combined unlikely hybrid monsters: animals with serpent's tails, fish with animal heads, and others found in medieval bestiaries. No less imaginative in his images of vegetation, he placed among the strange flora in his "pleasure" garden images of humans imprisoned in glass bubbles, suggesting that the magic garden fantasy is deeply embedded

in the human psyche as both pleasant dream and recurrent nightmare.

Hieronymous Bosch lived in a time that did not distinguish between art and craft. He painted altarpieces and panels for wealthy clients, but he also designed stained glass, jewelry, furniture, and even grotesque carnival masks. Some of Bosch's images have uncanny echoes in Chihuly's structures. There are, for example, glass towers in Bosch's garden of delights, as well as in his scene of hell in his depiction of the Last Judgment in another altarpiece. The shapes of Bosch's glass globes recall the vials used in alchemy, a popular medieval pursuit dedicated to turning base metal into gold. Because it involves a change in the physical state of matter—from molten liquid to hard crystal—the art of glassblowing is by its nature related to the alchemical experiments of the past. And in one sense it is precisely this metamorphic magical quality that appeals to Chihuly's sensibility. The idea of being a magician has always fascinated him. When Henry Geldzahler, then curator at the Metropolitan Museum of Art and one of Chihuly's earliest admirers, asked the artist to whom he felt closest, his answer was Houdini.

The grotesque fantasy and intricacy of Gothic filigree are visibly recalled in the tangle of tendrils in Chihuly's *Peacock Blue Tower* in the Garfield Park Conservatory. The organic formation of the *Peacock Blue Tower* is related to the *Temple of the Sun*, which Chihuly made for the entrance to Atlantis, the Bahamaian resort complex that features a great underwater aquarium. Other installations at the Chicago conservatory recall the various ones brought together in 1995 in the mega-production *Chihuly Over Venice*, when he transformed the entire Renaissance

lagoon city into an outdoor glass museum.

More than a dozen of Chihuly's *Ikebana* and *Venetians* are thoughtfully placed throughout the conservatory. Ikebana is the classic form of Japanese flower arrangement based on a refined and reductive aesthetic. As usual, Chihuly gives tradition a fresh interpretation. As he recalls, "Ben Moore organized the teams with Lino Tagliapietra as the maestro. We would bring together anywhere from twelve to eighteen glassblowers and try to do the most extreme pieces that I imagined they would be willing to do. Each session would get more elaborate. The teams kept getting bigger and wilder, and the pieces became more extreme. I would make a drawing and Lino would look at it and shout out a few orders. . . . One thing led to another."

This seemingly casual, one-thing-led-to-another approach underlies the organic way in which Chihuly works. The stimulus-response nature of his imagination requires constant new challenges to enable him to mutate new forms and techniques that expand the repertoire of both the artist and the medium. Chihuly's taste for exploration and adventure explains why his lifestyle is that of the itinerant nomad. Like the earthwork and site-specific artists and artistic teams such as Christo and Jean Claude, and Claes Oldenburg and Coosje van Bruggen, Chihuly travels the globe in search of stimulating projects that ultimately involve large numbers of other workers. Here the similarity ends, however, because Chihuly interacts with artisans with specialized skills, many of whom he has trained himself. Like his close friend the late Italo Scanga, Chihuly is an inspiring teacher who encourages individuality. For example, Howard Ben Tré and

Roni Horn have been among his many students.

In Japan, Chihuly sought out the last living master of blown-glass fishing floats, a traditional Japanese craft that is dying out. The original floats Chihuly made in Japan were simple spheres and glass bubbles. As the size of Chihuly's *Niijima Floats* increased, so did the installations. He was fascinated with glass floats both because of their association with water and because they are sculptural forms rather than containers or vessels. Tentatively explored by the resident koi fish, the *Fern Room Niijima Floats* at Garfield Park Conservatory float in and are nestled around the lushly edged pond. The floats are among the largest and most technically difficult things he has done, and they include spheres up to forty inches in diameter.

In their environmental scale, the seemingly floating "water lilies" in the Garfield *Persian Pond* installation have ancestors in the *Niijima Floats*. In the Garfield Park Conservatory context, the blossoms on the *Persian Pond* evoke Claude Monet's gardens in Giverny. They are a witty inversion of Monet's transplantation of real water lilies to a pretend Japanese garden based in turn on the Japanese woodcuts that inspired Monet's paintings. Chihuly's brilliant yellow forms, on the other hand, reflect real light and color, as opposed to translating them into highlights on canvas. This triple inversion, with its multiple implicit referents, lends the *Persian Pond* installation particular piquancy.

The installation at Garfield Park Conservatory comes almost four decades after Chihuly's first installations, done in 1966 while he was still a student at the University of Wisconsin. In his essentially site-specific but also tender ephemeral earthworks at Artpark, the artist used transparent plate glass, brilliant

neon, and ice. In the 1980s, he returned to installation art, and gradually his installations became architectural assemblages, ultimately leading to the often-huge chandeliers of hundreds of glass pieces put together with teams of assistants. In 1992, the Seattle Art Museum exhibited the first of these astonishing chandeliers.

The assemblage aesthetic common to avant-garde sculpture of the 1960s undoubtedly informs Chihuly's work as well. Chihuly has a degree in sculpture, and his knowledge has served him well in designing the armatures to which an infinite combination of glass parts are attached. The emphasis on technology, as well as the interest in site-specific installations, also connects him to his generation, which came of age in the 1960s. The *Chandeliers* can be seen as science-fiction adaptations of the classical Venetian fixtures that decorate the great palazzi of the Grand Canal. Hung

outdoors, they suggest the extravagance and luxury of the Hanging Gardens of Babylon, one of the seven wonders of the ancient world. These great crystalline constructions can weigh as much as 2,500 pounds, and, through time, the hundreds of individual glass pieces attached to steel armatures have become increasingly phantasmagoric. The image of an explosion of crystals is decidedly contemporary as well as central to Chihuly's personal style.

Blurring art categories is another legacy of the experimental spirit of the 1960s. Often the most dramatic changes are recognized only in retrospect. Hieronymous Bosch, for example, was still a member of a guild, but his Italian contemporary Leonardo da Vinci was preaching the autonomy and superiority of painting as a strictly conceptual art. Today, the elimination of the distinctions between the "uselessness" of high art and

the "usefulness" of furniture, vessels, and porcelain has erased the distinction between the fine and decorative arts, proclaiming autonomy and individual expressiveness as the right of the sculptors who use clay or glass as material as much as of the painter. By the same token, photography and film, formerly considered minor arts, are now on equal footing with the "major" arts.

After several decades of interdisciplinary art, the division between art and craft, like that between the major and minor arts, now seems dead. No one asks any longer if ceramists Robert Arneson, Kenneth Price, or Peter Voulkos are sculptors. What they have done for clay, Chihuly has done for glass. Indeed, he has gone even further in reconciling what has been thought of as a craft material by making entire installations in glass that go beyond sculpture into architecture.

Chihuly could not himself have broken through so many of these boundaries if he were not a voyager in the broadest sense. The only way to understand the meanderings of Chihuly's life is as an odyssey, an adventure of discovery. Part Homer's wandering Odysseus and part Ken Kesey's Merry Prankster, he took a minor art and reinterpreted it through conventions of major art of the avant-garde, without sacrificing what made historical art exciting and popular. His reinterpretation of tradition and his admixtures of disciplines and conventions are characteristics of the most significant art of our time, from Jasper Johns's and Robert Rauschenberg's symbiosis of painting with printmaking to Frank Stella's recombinations of printmaking with painting projected to an architectural scale as theatrical decor.

Chihuly's road to mastery of his medium and the

development of personal style took many unexpected turns. In 1961, at age twenty, he wrote a term paper on Vincent van Gogh and first melted and fused stained glass as a naive experiment while a student at the University of Washington in Seattle. In 1965, he began experimenting on his own in his basement studio and blew his first glass bubble by melting that stained glass and using a metal pipe. To earn money for graduate school, he worked as a fisherman in Alaska the following year and then won a full scholarship to the graduate school of the University of Wisconsin at Madison, where Harvey Littleton had started the first glass program in the United States.

In many respects, Littleton played a similar role to that of June Wayne, who set up the Tamarind workshop to train the first American master printers in the European tradition. Up until 1957–58, when Littleton visited the island of Murano, the traditional techniques of Venetian glassblowing were well-guarded secrets within the clannish glassblowing community in Venice.

Chihuly studied glassblowing with Littleton and received a master's degree in sculpture in 1967 from Wisconsin. He decided to enroll at the prestigious Rhode Island School of Design (RISD) in Providence, and there he began his experiments in outdoor works using neon, argon, and blown glass. At RISD he received a prestigious Louis Comfort Tiffany Foundation Grant for work in glass.

The turning point in Chihuly's life came in 1968, when he was awarded a Fulbright Fellowship to study in Venice. He was able to learn the traditional techniques of Venetian glassblowing, but, above all, he absorbed a spirit of teamwork, which inspired him to return to the United States to train teams of young artisans

and to grow and improvise along with them.

While Venice was a first love, Chihuly also loves Ireland (his own background is Hungarian and Czech on his father's side and Swedish and Norwegian on his mother's). At times he has displayed the leprechaun's mischievousness, ignoring rules and jumping over boundaries. However, he understands that to break the rules, you first have to know what they are. His discoveries made after fully mastering various disciplines recall the words of painter John Graham: "No tradition, no revolution." Having mastered the tradition, he is now in a position to transform it.

Chihuly's extravagant sensibility has antecedents in nineteenth-century Romanticism. His fantastic shimmering spectacles recall Samuel Taylor Coleridge's description of the stately pleasure palace of Kubla Khan in Xanadu. The tales of the German Romantic author and composer E.T.A. Hoffmann are another example of the Gothic imagination that feeds from Romanticism to Surrealism and science fiction. All have in common a taste for the marvelous and the unearthly—what the German Romantics called the *Unheimlich*, or the uncanny. Chihuly's style as it evolved has become increasingly supernatural and Romantic, filling more and more space with delirious decoration worthy of Gustav Klimt's Viennese Secession architectural projects.

Chihuly himself refuses to assume intellectual postures or to theorize about his thinking. There is a major element of fantasy in Chihuly's work that separates him from the literalness of minimal art. For this reason, his work stands in contrast to contemporary currents of art such as site-specificity of earthworks and the literalness of minimal art, which requires that what was once illusory in painting and

sculpture like light, color, and shape now becomes literal and united. On the other hand, his work seeks to resolve a perpetual problem for modernist painting. Ever since Thomas Wilfred invented the Lumia Box, a light box filled with changing colors, the idea that the canvas support needed somehow to become transparent to free color and light from materialism has haunted painting.

The dream of disembodied color and form floating on a transparent ground has been a common thread in modern painting as it sought to become increasingly abstracted from matter. Marcel Duchamp, in his *Large Glass*, resolved the problem of suspended forms in space by inlaying metallic forms into transparent glass, but he did not deal with the problem of color. Jackson Pollock's painting on glass was an attempt to render the support transparent so that drawing would seem to be suspended in air. The painting was an experiment made for Hans Namuth's 1951 film of Pollock painting. Pollock himself did not repeat the effort, but one senses when seeing videos of Chihuly working that he was influenced by Namuth's film. Namuth revealed how Pollock's pouring, spilling, and spattering "drip" process became the permanent record on canvases of an immediate and spontaneous, though controlled, experience. The idea that intuition and spontaneity should not be obstructed is an article of faith for Chihuly. Increasingly he has come to emphasize that glass takes on its permanent form gradually; its shape can be modified during the process of its creation.

Every aspect of Chihuly's creativity was tested in 1995, when he embarked on the major multifaceted international project *Chihuly Over Venice*. He worked in

glass factories in Finland, Ireland, and Mexico, and the resultant sculptures were installed over the canals and piazzas of Venice. Revisiting Venice, where he had begun his career as an apprentice, Chihuly, now a mature master, set out to prove that glass not only can take on architectural dimension, it can also transform outdoor space. Festooning the canals with chandeliers that took the conventions of the fixtures inside the palazzi to cinematic proportions, he magically reversed interior and exterior.

The preparations for his triumphant return to Venice began in Nuutajärvi, Finland. Then he and his team traveled to the Waterford factory in Ireland, famous for fine crystal, before moving on to Monterrey, Mexico, where popular colored glass is produced. In Venice in 1996, he combined the disparate talents of his team to assemble the cumulative shipments arriving from Mexico, Ireland, and Finland. The shapes were as unexpected and varied as forms found in nature. The history of the material, from molten liquid to permanent solid, is preserved in the organic crystalline and large sculptures.

Four years after Venice, Chihuly assembled what was up to that time his most ambitious and complex installations, *Chihuly in the Light of Jerusalem 2000*. More than a million people visited the installations within the stone walls of the Tower of David Museum of the History of Jerusalem. As a thank-you to the people of Jerusalem, he also created a sixty-four-ton *Wall of Ice* echoing the ancient walls, and he hoped tensions there might melt away as his ice wall did—in three days.

For all of his projects, including the most ambitious such as Venice and Jerusalem, Chihuly has always

started with drawings that give the general sense of the look and concept of the work to be produced by the studio. In making his drawings, he stands above a surface that is laid on the ground, working as Pollock did, directly from the tube of pigment or spattering and pouring. From these spontaneous sketches, he and assistants begin to blow glass elements that will eventually be assembled in the large-scale installations. He combines professionalism with play, and the results are both delightfully playful and impressively professional.

Chihuly works with the environment and the site, and the forms come out of the process of that interaction. He claims to "listen to the glass" in order to take best advantage of its capacities to permit color to fade and disappear into pure light. He brings a pragmatic American attitude about speed, efficiency, and technological innovation to an ancient art form in order to create miraculous new effects.

Chihuly has no set of rigid or prior rules. Clearly he is amused by his creations, and his intention is to share this pleasure with others. There is an element of "action painting," and he is convinced that materials discover artists, not vice versa. He operates like the medieval master builder, depending on teams of artisans to realize his overall concept while permitting them liberties of personal interpretation that destroy uniformity and repetition. He does not seek perfection but the expression of energy, both his own and that of his team. "The more I do," he says, "the more I can do. I take ideas from everybody and ultimately draw my own conclusion. I don't think, I just work, and I try to do what feels right."

Chihuly's magical mystery tour has taken him

from objects to environments, from inside to outside, from decoration to revelation. The shapes that are created or discovered become as unexpected and varied as natural forms. The history of the material from its molten liquid to its solid state is preserved in Chihuly's forms, giving his glass pieces a contemporary inflection. He twists and bends eccentric shapes, which grow complex and quirky, wildly imaginative and often contradictory in their forms and functions.

Even at home in Seattle, Chihuly is everywhere at once. Like a coach cheering on the team, he instructs, cajoles, directs, and encourages individual interpretation of the thousands of elements that make up the installations he has conceived. In the studio, the sound system alternates songs from the Beatles' *Sgt. Pepper* album with arias from Italian opera.

In *City of Glass*, novelist Paul Auster describes the fantasy of a crystal city. Chihuly appears to be gearing up to realize that fantasy. He is about to realize yet another correlation between glass and water in his tour de force for the entry to Tacoma, Washington's new Museum of Glass. The *Chihuly Bridge of Glass* will form a pedestrian link between downtown Tacoma's Pacific Avenue and the new museum. The bridge's 500-foot span includes effects that are lavish and powerful. "I do what I feel like doing," Chihuly explains. "I don't think about good or bad taste, or politically correct strategies." One has the sense that what Chihuly really seeks to do is to surprise himself.

There are periods when revolutionary personalities, because of their ethical rejection of human bloodshed, cannot express themselves in actual revolutions. This is essentially what happened to the generation of 1968, whose most irresponsible members chose terrorism while

its finest minds turned to art and other creative modalities that they hoped would change the world. Whether, in the end, their public projects and ephemeral installations are more than diversions or advertisements for their sponsors, it is too soon to say. However, we can see that they represent a rebirth of the forms of festivities that brought the works of the great masters of art, design, theater, and opera to the public as part of the outdoor festivals that medieval lords shared with their subjects.

Today, scholars are finally turning their attention from the so-called major art forms—painting, sculpture, and architecture—to elucidate the significant historical role of the "luxury arts": the tapestries, embroideries, jewelry, and furniture designs, as well as the ephemeral multimedia spectacles that were their public parallel.

The destruction of hierarchies among the arts and of the line separating the fine arts from guild crafts may strike a blow at Leonardo da Vinci's theories, but it may also reflect larger currents in today's global culture. This emergent global culture demands grand scale and impressive installations as symbols of cities, institutions, and enterprises. These projects reflect not the Renaissance view of the individual genius agonizing in isolation but rather the collective projects of the Middle Ages that were, as it turned out, far more democratic. It is more than possible that ours is a moment that once again, for various social, cultural, political, and economic reasons, permits forms of artisanship to combine with painting, sculpture, and architecture in dramatic collective communal undertakings under the direction of a master builder.

Certainly an artist like Dale Chihuly is at the

forefront of this new fusion of the arts and of the arts with technology. Yet when he speaks of his work, there is something of the innocent expression on the face of the boy in Jean-Baptiste-Siméon Chardin's famous painting of the *Boy Blowing Bubbles*. Blowing bubbles is, of course, a metaphor for dreaming. Dale Chihuly has made the bubbles real and tangible in fantasy environments that delight and enchant in ways that stimulate others to dream.

A Garden of Glass   Lisa C. Roberts

Imagine a garden of glass, planted under glass, nestled among lacy ferns, soaring palms, spiny cacti, and fruiting bananas. To see Dale Chihuly's magnificent artwork displayed amid the plant kingdom from which so many of his forms seem to emanate is to see both art and plants in a new light. Each reflects the other in a shimmery mix of tendrils, buds, and fronds. The fact that this dance takes place within the walls of a historic glasshouse makes it that much more resonant, as though someone had subverted the boundaries between the house and its leafy occupants.

And why not? Conservatories are, after all, exquisitely crafted re-creations of natural environments. Introducing Chihuly's glasswork takes the manipulation to another level, one that aspires to stimulation, not simulation. It startles expectation, stretches the imagination, and provides a new way of experiencing both plants and art.

There was a time when conservatories did just that, providing an experience that was not just new but a leap from people's daily lives. Tropical plants were strange, exotic, and richly evocative of faraway lands. Conservatories were places of refuge and recreation, where people could indulge romantic fantasies about nature and the world. Those fantasies were enhanced by the manner in which plants were exhibited.

This was especially true in the nineteenth century, an age of great exploration and widespread collecting. It

was not uncommon to find plants displayed alongside animals, artifacts, and other curios from newly discovered lands. Music and artwork also found their way into conservatory settings, which provided an idyllic venue for cultural pursuits. In many ways, Chihuly's installations hark back to these precedents. He has resurrected, in a beautiful and seemingly effortless way, what was once an easy union between the muses of culture and horticulture.

Conservatories have their origin in horticultural practice. Glasshouses, greenhouses, hothouses, orangeries, winter gardens, crystal palaces, Dutch stoves, German floras—their forms have varied throughout history, but they were all created for one basic purpose: to shelter plants from the cold. Since antiquity, growers have sought to gain the upper hand over nature's seasons and their insistent cycles. The result has been the invention of a series of structures designed to ward off the elements and optimize growing conditions by controlling the temperature, light, and humidity. Glass was key to their evolution, as it was solid enough to enclose a microclimate but transparent enough to allow life-giving light to pass.

It was not until the nineteenth century that glasshouses, as they were known, came to play a large role in social and cultural life. By this time, they were common in botanical gardens and universities, where they were primarily used for cultivating, studying, and experimenting with newly discovered plants. They had also become an accessory of the landed gentry, built on private estates for the purpose of growing the exotic and sometimes tender plants that some aristocrat had brought back from foreign travels. Often extensions of the home itself, it was only a matter of time before

private glasshouses were used by family residents for reading, strolling, and entertaining. This was a social function that was markedly non-horticultural. It changed the way plants were treated forever, as they took on a much wider universe of meaning and significance.

No longer were plants simply horticultural specimens. They were also something to be experienced: decorative props, eccentric curiosities, totems of paradisiacal isles and conquered lands. While their botanical aspects remained paramount among students of the plant kingdom, their symbolic aspects were embraced by men and women of leisure.

This fact had its own redolent symbolism. Because large, heated glasshouses could be afforded only by a privileged class of people, they came to signify a certain exalted stature in society. The aristocracy often collected or purchased entire plant collections, much as early art collectors might amass paintings or sculptures. As glass and iron technology advanced, private glasshouses grew in size to the point that they became detached from the living quarters. By the mid-nineteenth century, conservatories dotted Europe, each outdoing the last with elaborately designed interiors that included streams, fountains, birds, fish, waterfalls, and statues. King Ludwig II of Bavaria went so far as to install a small lake with a boat, a fisherman's hut, a silk tent, a kiosk, and a painted vista of the Himalayas. Others introduced into their spaces garden furniture, divans, candelabra, and oriental carpets, creating a kind of salon for relaxation and entertaining.

At the same time that private glasshouses were proliferating, a new type of glass building began to appear for the general public. "Winter gardens" incorporated

social spaces as diverse as cafés, art galleries, and libraries. The plants were largely embellishments to recreational activities such as concerts, billiards, reading, eating, even dancing. Men could smoke and play cards, and people would promenade amid the plants, perhaps even listening to music and poetry.

Entertainment may have been the focus here, but the plants were what made it all work. People wanted to relax in a setting that gave relief from the crowded, overbuilt city outside, particularly during the winter months when the light was poor and the weather cold. In some winter gardens, the effect of the greenery was enhanced by adding objets d'art, butterflies, songbirds, and even caged beasts.

Meanwhile, glasshouses continued to evolve in association with botanical gardens and horticultural societies to support a scientific mission. Plants in these settings were arranged in a more systematic manner that took into account their botanical families or habitats. Many establishments opened their doors to the public, given the important social function that the great winter gardens had come to play. It is probably here that a happy medium was struck between the interests of science and those of the public, and this model was widely adopted by North American public conservatories.

The earliest public conservatories in the United States appeared in the later nineteenth century and included Garfield Park Conservatory. First constructed in 1886, Garfield's original building was one of several conservatories established in the major parks ringing Chicago, including Lincoln, Humboldt, Garfield, Douglas, Washington, and Jackson parks. It was later razed, along with the Humboldt and Douglas Park

Conservatories, and a huge, centralized facility was erected in their place. Opened in 1908, the new Garfield Park Conservatory was the largest in the world, the vision of celebrated landscape architect and then parks superintendent Jens Jensen.

Jensen's ideas for the great conservatory were considered revolutionary at the time. Bucking the Victorian tradition of displaying plants in groupings of pots, he designed each room as a natural-looking landscape. It was not the first time plants had been placed directly into the soil, but Jensen made the practice his signature, taking care to place stonework, lagoons, and plants to mask the mechanical structures supporting them and create the illusion of a natural setting. So effective was his artistry that visitors to the newly opened Fern Room marveled at the feat of erecting a glass structure over an existing lagoon.

Twentieth-century conservatories have largely followed this tradition. Plant collections are usually organized for public display according to botanically based themes such as plant family, native origin, or habitat, and they are exhibited in pleasing, scenic arrangements that mimic nature. Most try to balance their scientific and public dimensions, and many have made education a central part of their mission. The experience they impart, however, has changed from days gone by—in part a function of the fact that they now inhabit a changed world.

Today, mass media and world travel have brought the farthest corners of the globe within reach, making the strange increasingly familiar. While conservatories still present unfamiliar plants with which many people have had no direct contact, they also contain things about which most people have a variety of images and

references. The environmental movement has turned rain forests and other endangered habitats into current affairs. Palm trees, coconuts, and saguaros have taken root in popular culture and are widely portrayed in cartoons, travel brochures, movies, and advertising. Commercial ventures from the Banana Republic to the Rainforest Café have borrowed heavily from images of tropical havens to fuel people's fantasies of exploration and adventure.

The result is that conservatories are no longer experienced in quite the same way as their nineteenth-century predecessors. Their power now comes not so much from their presentation of the strange as from their embodiment of the real. In a culture that has perfected the art of simulation, where people can experience pyramids in Las Vegas and safari at Disney, and where nature has been re-created everywhere from restaurants to theme parks to museum exhibits, conservatories stand apart in their preservation of the real thing. Living plants grow and die. Banana trees fruit, flowers bloom and fade, leaves curl. Pests fight for a stronghold as they munch their way through their own culinary nirvana. The whole thing is alive, imperfect, and real.

The presumption, of course, is that all of this reality truly represents what is real. Conservatories may look and feel like the real thing, but they are still re-creations of something even more original—namely, rain forests, deserts, and ponds that exist naturally in the world. Their power lies in the accuracy of the reproduction, built, as it is, of living plants, fertile soil, and craggy rocks. It is a supreme artistry in its own right, whose medium happens to be the stuff of nature.

Now, into all this reality, Dale Chihuly has

introduced his arresting and lustrous forms. And suddenly the point is not reality but enchantment. Magic. Pure, heart-stopping beauty. And not just the artwork, which is dazzling unto itself. The plants themselves are transformed by their new neighbors so that viewers see nature in a whole new light. It is a remarkable achievement, a throwback to former days when conservatories presented people with a sight that was utterly new.

What is so novel here? Why is this display enthralling nearly every visitor who comes to see it? Beauty has fallen out of favor in recent years, though we would never admit it. We think we value it, but what gets put forth in this culture is usually about something else, such as fashion, design, or entertainment. So to encounter something of true beauty—however that may strike one—can be a deeply moving experience.

Somehow, this seems to have been achieved at the conservatory by bringing plants and glass together in a blurring of boundaries. Two things that are so essentially different—one animate, the other inanimate; one pliable and textured, the other hard and shiny; one natural, the other cultural—come together and turn our expectations on their heads. Long-standing categories mingle together: gallery and greenhouse; exhibit and garden; art and nature. The result is that one begins to see with new eyes.

We now suddenly notice what a vast range of greens nature presents when her foliage is juxtaposed with a vast range of glassy yellows. Or how straight and upright is the stance of a banana tree, a grove of soldiers standing at attention, which becomes apparent when interspersed with a regiment of straight, upright glass rods. And that the effect works both ways, so that in

another setting, those same glass rods reflect the character of the plants, bringing to mind the prickly spines of the cacti surrounding them.

There is also the matter of language, how names alter what we see. By discovering that the rods are actually called *Reeds*, a far more botanical designation, we are introduced to a completely different yet fitting image. We read the name *Macchia Forest*, and conjure an image to the eye of an understory—in this case, of brightly colored vessels.

There are also the unnamed pieces, the bulbous onions, curly tendrils, and arching stalks that emerge colorfully and gracefully from within the foliage, and whose forms are so essentially organic that they seem to belong there, side by side with the plants.

In the end, we have been treated to a feast of the eyes, and never again will we look at either Chihuly or plants in quite the same way.

So why is this important? Why is it valued? Why are people walking away saying this is an experience not to be missed? And how does it further our purpose as a conservatory?

Conservatories in this day and age have multiple identities which rest, in the main, on two key activities: collecting and exhibiting plants. Some conservatories do research; Garfield does not. Ours is a wholly public endeavor. We educate, establish community relations, and give out technical advice. We are a display garden and a party palace. We do it all because we love plants, and believe that they are central to what life is all about.

That is quite a claim—but the fact is, we could not live without plants. Plants are the basis of life itself. They produce our food, our medicine, and the oxygen that we breathe. They are a source of artistic

inspiration and religious symbolism. They even gave rise to new forms of life, as plants evolved into animals and, in turn, ourselves.

Is it any wonder that people have made the conservatory into a site of ritual and ceremony, where wedding vows are exchanged, life events celebrated, holiday pilgrimages made? Every holiday has its pilgrims to the conservatory. For that matter, every day finds its pilgrims—people in search of a certain kind of place or experience that the conservatory satisfies.

This is an aspect of the conservatory that is profoundly spiritual in nature, and that appeals to people's most primal instincts and needs. This is perhaps the hardest identity to tease out, yet in some ways it is fundamental to all the others. It has to do with the spark ignited in one's heart by the experience of engaging with plants and making some personal connection. It may be an aesthetic appreciation, it may be a personal insight, it may be new information. It is what makes people care about plants and want them in their lives. And it is something that is deeply affective in nature.

It is not something, however, that conservatories find easy to address. Typically they have defined and interpreted their collections in botanical, horticultural, or ecological terms. Plant sciences constitute their dominant paradigm and standard of discourse. Yet visitors' primary experiences tend to be affective, not cognitive; they are as quick to report on how they feel as on what they learned. When they enter a conservatory they stop, linger, wander, inhale, and relax. It is because of this that Garfield Park Conservatory has made a central feature of its mission, "providing a

botanical haven in the city." For many people, that's what the conservatory is. A green sanctuary where they can get away and recharge. A place to slow down, converse, ponder life.

It would follow that activities of display and interpretation need to be developed to support this aspect, to treat the plant collections in a way that heightens their affective as opposed to their scientific qualities. What better tool for such treatment than the arts? After all, the arts by their nature have deep roots in the affective part of the mind. And really, plants are as much about art as they are about science.

This notion, of course, is hardly new. It stands at the core of the work of gardeners and designers who arrange plants into artful displays. It has roots in the winter gardens of bygone days when plants mixed freely with the arts. It is the governing precept of a handful of contemporary artists who take as their medium plants and other natural elements. And it is the fundamental notion behind Chihuly's elegant garden under glass.

However, Chihuly has achieved something that goes beyond easy categories. It's not just that art has been juxtaposed with plants, or that art is mimicking plants, or even that art has anything in particular to do with plants. It's that art and plants have been brought together in a way in which both are transformed. And the conservatory itself is transformed. And a synergy is released that appeals directly to the affective realm. No wonder people respond. In a funny way, Chihuly has taken the real and made it even more real. Not by improving the simulation, but by drawing out the essence. This is his gift. This is our fortune. A garden of glass. . . .

Chihuly under Glass   Mark McDonnell

This exhibition at the Garfield Park Conservatory in Chicago gives us another context in which to consider Dale Chihuly's installations. He has increasingly challenged preconceived notions of how and where art can be exhibited. Long a veteran of exhibiting in the "white boxes" of the museum world, he has increasingly sought opportunities to take his work outside, into the realm of public art spaces, and out into the landscape.

"I want my work to look like it just happened, as if it was made by nature."   Dale Chihuly

Chihuly has installed his work on the wall, on the floor, overhead, on roofs, and in courtyards, and he has hung his work from every place imaginable. He has worked in the Jacobean garden of a castle in Lismore, Ireland; the bucolic gardens at LongHouse on Long Island, New York; a country estate in Vianne, France; and even the vineyards of Napa Valley, California. He has worked in the rivers and forests of Finland, the deserts of Mexico, the beaches and mountains of Japan, and the snow of his native Cascade Mountains in the Pacific Northwest. Major projects have included chandelier installations sited in and around the canals of Venice, and a monumental site-specific installation inside the stone walls of the ancient Citadel in the Old City of Jerusalem. He has set his glass underwater,

in lap pools, in fountains, and frozen in blocks of ice, and he has worked with plant materials in dozens of situations. On occasion he has simply thrown his objects into the water, leaving them to float freely. It seems that no place escapes him as he tirelessly continues to search out new possibilities.

"Without a glass palace, life becomes a burden."
Paul Scheerbart

Chihuly has a lifelong fascination with transparency in architecture and has a thorough knowledge of glasshouse history and glass architecture. As a young professor at the Rhode Island School of Design, he immersed himself in the library's rare-book collection. There he noticed a first edition of Raymond McGrath and

A.C. Frost's 1937 classic, *Glass in Architecture and Decoration*, which illustrates clearly and concisely the origins and development of the glasshouse through essays and extraordinary photographs. Both *Glass Architecture* by the German poet Paul Scheerbart (1914) and *Alpine Architecture* by the visionary architect Bruno Taut (1919) also caught Chihuly's attention. Scheerbart and Taut shared the dream of living in a world of glass architecture in which cities encapsulated by glass domes contained glasshouses and public palaces appointed with glass furniture. Taut eventually founded the Glass Chain, a secret society of Germany's leading architects. Using pen names, they shared their utopian vision of the future, corresponding with one another and passing around their sketches of glass architecture. They regarded the nineteenth-century iron-and-glass

WINDMILL PALM
Trachycarpus fortunei
Palmae
China, Japan

West Indian Holly
coccinea
Leeaceae
Burma

horticultural and exhibition buildings as ideal for human habitation. They truly believed that through this new glass architecture, they could elevate culture. They dreamed of living in crystalline structures, employing air balloons to aid in their construction. They called for the end of the window, as buildings from now on were to be completely clad in glass.

The prophetic ideals of a glass culture as proposed by Scheerbart, Taut, and others, illustrating the true potential of the glass medium, have inspired Chihuly and subsequently an entire generation of his students. Chihuly has visited notable glasshouses and glass buildings in Europe and North America during his frequent travels. He possesses an extensive collection of books, photographs, and vintage hand-colored postcards of glasshouses, some of which appear in this publication.

Chihuly has also created installations in conservatories other than Garfield. In 1995 he placed cut-crystal shapes in the vinery that Joseph Paxton designed in the 1860s for the duke of Devonshire's hunting estate at Lismore Castle in Ireland. Later that year, Chihuly installed a more ambitious project at the restored Curvilinear Range, one of the glasshouses at the National Botanical Gardens in Glasnevin, Ireland. This architectural jewel was designed and built by William Turner in 1843. In 2000, Chihuly went to Australia to work at various sites including the Palm House, which was designed by the architect Gustav Runge; built in Bremen, Germany, in 1875; and then shipped and erected at the Adelaide Botanical Gardens.

"Exuberance is beauty."   William Blake

This brings us to Garfield Park Conservatory. Designed by the landscape architect Jens Jensen in 1908, it remains the largest extant glasshouse in North America. His design for the building is said to mimic haystacks seen in the flat landscape of rural Illinois. Garfield hosts a world-class plant collection. This venue presents an opportunity to see Chihuly's work in this inspired setting.

The separate reality of the glasshouse allows the visitor to interact casually, refocus, and have some time for introspection. Its tranquil environment includes warmth, moisture, the sweet smell of soil, the sound of moving water, and atmospheric light. Chihuly—always the keen observer of light—has fully exploited its transience. Special lighting in the conservatory and extended hours provide a different experience at night. No two visits are ever the same.

Few artists would choose to work within a dense environment of competing plants or in a conservatory, much less succeed so effectively. The plants and glass enjoy a comfortable symbiosis, remaining equals. Chihuly has exploited the close relationship of the off-center liquid organic quality of glass and the nature of the plants in this collection. He introduced contrasting colors, bold and deliberate, and magnified the scale of his work to meet the largess of the building. Sensual organic glass forms are casually installed among complementing growing forms. Shortly after his initial installation, Chihuly's excitement about the exhibition led to his return, bringing back with him more glass to add to the space.

Chihuly is a most eloquent, evenhanded director and editor, leaving us to discover a new

DOUBLE COCONUT
Lodoicea maldivica
Palmae
Seychelles Island,
Indian Ocean

indigenous species—glass. This exhibition, *Chihuly in the Park: A Garden of Glass*, offers a special opportunity to see Chihuly's thoughtful and joyful exploration of glass among exuberant plants, in a building worthy of his attention, in what is the most sublime environment possible . . . under glass.

GARDENS

& GLASS

People often ask me why I work with glass, and how I got started. I never know really the answer to why, because I don't start from reasons. I began from a fascination with glass itself. 1998

Glassblowing is a spontaneous medium that suits me. It requires split-second decisions and a great team. It's very athletic. The more you blow, the better you get. I've been at it for thirty-six years and am as infatuated as when I blew my first bubble in 1965 in my basement in South Seattle.

In 1981 I started working on the *Macchia*. It was color (often bright, strange, mostly opaque, where the outside

was dramatically contrasted with the inside) that we were concerned with. Most people don't realize it, but blowing a piece that combines a range of colors is extremely difficult. Each color attracts and holds the heat differently. It turns out that size is extremely important to the *Macchias*. With them I felt for the first time that a piece of glass held its own in a room. 1 9 8 6

It's possible to spend several hours blowing a piece of glass, but traditionally five or ten or fifteen minutes would be the more likely time it took to make something. We push this up to, let's say, maybe an hour of working on a piece. But basically an hour's not very long, and boom! It's over, done. That's the way I like to work. Fast, quick, and I like to do a lot in a day.

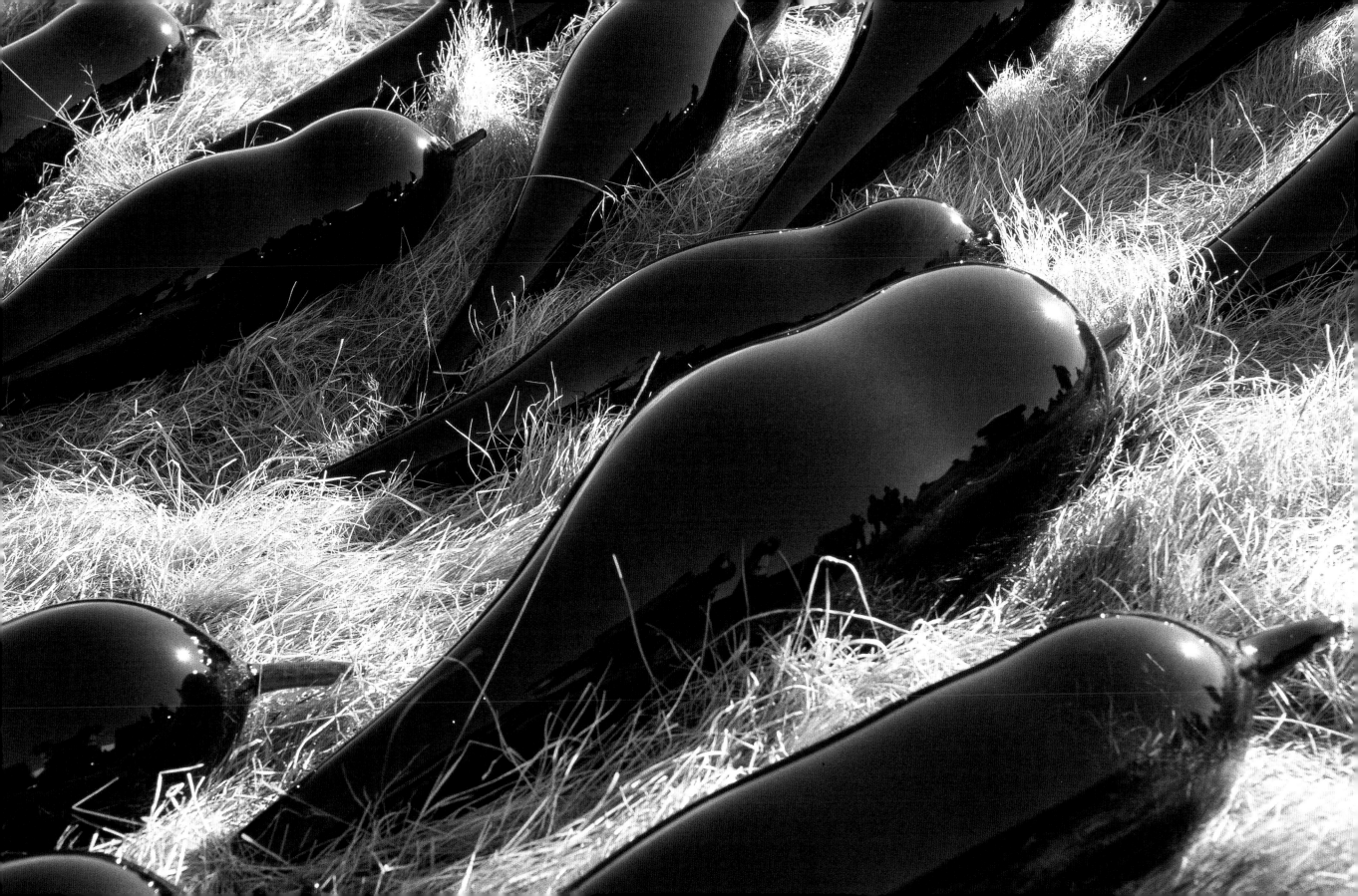

I had to come up with a name for the series. And I called my friend Italo Scanga. I said, "Italo, what does spotted mean in Italian?" . . . and he said, "'*Macchia*,' which comes from 'immaculate,' meaning 'unspotted.'" I liked the whole connection of the word macchia. It also meant 'patina,' and it meant 'to sketch,' and it also had a lot of artistic roots to it. 1 9 9 2

I made the first *Chandelier* in 1992 for the Seattle Art Museum. It was a big show, the entire second floor, and there was an area that wasn't working. At the last minute, I had the glassblowers start making a very simple shape— one of the easiest forms one can blow. It is also strong and simple, and I knew it would hang well. I put ten or fifteen blowers on the project, and we made it in a few days and then hung it immediately in the museum without first making a mock-up. It was a little risky, but I was very

confident. I put a large black granite table, eight by eight feet, under the piece to keep viewers back and to have a reflection. 1996

What makes the *Chandeliers* work for me is the massing of color. If you take hundreds or thousands of blown pieces of one color, put them together, and then shoot light through them, now that's going to be something to look at! When you hang it in space, it becomes mysterious, defying gravity, becoming something you have never seen before. 1996

I began drawing so the gaffers (the guys in charge of the blow team) could see and understand the forms I wanted them to blow. I wanted the drawings to look like the glass, so I ended up using graphite and colored pencils by the fistfuls. I would draw on the steel marvering table

with bits of glass under the paper to give it a texture. For color, I used whatever I could find around the shop—tea, fruit juices, wine, coffee (my friend Italo's influence). There was a period when I was drinking a lot of seltzer with bitters—the bitters made a beautiful saffron color. Mercurochrome from the medicine kit made a great orange, but the bouquet wasn't as good as the bitters. 1988

Working with a team is good for me—new people, new ideas, new places. *Chihuly Over Venice* started out with the end in sight—which was the *Chandeliers* hanging over canals. But the people became more important. All the glassblowers and artisans from different countries working hand in hand with all the Americans. The hanging of the *Chandeliers* became secondary to the people interaction. 1996

With glassblowing, the only way to make it good is to do it over and over. It's a question of time. You just have to become one with the material and understand it. You can't see it; you have to feel it. And by doing it over and over and over, you begin to understand what it can do. You begin to develop forms and things begin to happen.

I was the first American glassblower who didn't do the work myself. I went on the road so people could see the process and understand. 1998

The technology really hasn't changed. . . . We use the same tools they used 2,000 years ago. The difference is that when I started, everyone wanted to control the blowing process. I just went with it. The natural elements of fire, movement, gravity, and centrifugal force were always there, and are always with us. The difference was that I

worked in this abstract way and could let the forces of nature have a bigger role in the ultimate shape. 1 9 9 5

Sometimes you see a great piece evolving, but you may lose it because glass is such a fragile material. . . . That's part of its magical beauty. 1 9 9 3

I've been such a nomad all my life, I don't think I'll ever lose the desire to travel to beautiful places—one more archipelago, another ring of standing stones, another glassblowing session in some exotic spot, or just one more trip to Venice to see the full moon over the Grand Canal. 1 9 8 6

It's interesting that the most difficult series I have ever blown are the *Floats*. Considering a sphere is the easiest form to make in glass, it's the most natural form

you could blow. But it's not natural at this scale. . . . I started the *Floats* in the odd way that many series have begun. I told Rich Royal and the team to blow as big a ball as they could and to put a dimple in the end so we could stick a smaller ball on top. 1992

Plastic is an extraordinary material. I think the problem people have with plastic is that it has no history (Italo told me that). Glass breaks, and that's an added attraction. At any moment it can disappear. 1997

I can't understand it when people say they don't like a particular color. . . . How on earth can you not like a color? 1996

I'm lucky that my work appeals to people of all ages. It's more accessible than most public work, which has to

do with the material. People for centuries have been fascinated with glass, colored or crystal, as it transmits light in a special way. At any moment it might break. It's magic. It's the most mysterious of all materials. People look at the glass and just wonder. 1 9 9 2

I tend to do things on a large scale because it's exciting; it's a technical challenge. I like to push things in new and different ways.

Glass can be transparent, translucent, or opaque. It can be sharp or smooth, strong or fragile. It has many different forms. The only other substance that has similar qualities is plastic, but you can't blow plastic. 1 9 9 6

I was making a drawing and there were a dozen pencils around. I wanted to fill in some part of the drawing.

Instead of using one pencil . . . it didn't take long to figure out that if you grabbed a dozen you could do it faster. Or if you grabbed fifty. I think I used to be able to hold about fifty pencils in one hand. 1 9 9 8

People ask me, "Are you born with this energy? Is it your history that allows it to come out in a way? Are you able to see the world in a different way?" I have to reply that I just don't know. 1 9 9 5

I delayed doing the project for Harriet Bullitt up in Leavenworth, which is in the snow of the Cascade Mountains. A little-known fact is that Mount Rainier often has the largest snowfall in the world, and the Cascade Mountains in general have vast snow levels. I think Mount Rainier, in a record year, will have a hundred feet of snow on top. So the time was up. I needed

to get the project going for Harriet. I just couldn't figure out a way to do it inside, in the lodge, that made sense. 1998

It's just a way of life for me to work with teams.

I love to juxtapose the man-made and the natural to make people wonder and ask, "Are they man-made or did they come from nature?" That's a very important part of my work. 1998

To watch Richie [Royal] blow out a *Macchia* is really something, because it remains very symmetrical, a ball about two feet in diameter, until the final heat. Then you go in, it gets hot, hotter, hotter, you have to move it faster, faster, and the ball begins to open, open, open, open, open, and open. It gets opened to about four feet.

Then you hold it down, and then the wrinkles and the forms take place. And much of that has to do with how the color was applied, and how the piece was blown. 1998

As a matter of fact, I think plastic and glass can sometimes be indistinguishable. 2000

I knew that if I made the baskets thin I could manipulate them more. First I would bang them with a paddle to beat them up a bit. But I soon learned that if I just used the heat of the furnace and the fire, I could get the same kind of movement from the fire itself, and it was more beautiful. 1995

The first piece of glass that was made at Pilchuck was a series of "floats" that Jamie [Carpenter] and I blew

together and sent off like soap bubbles to sail in the pond behind the glass shop. 1 9 9 2

I just love the word "Ikebana," so I used it. Many of the *Venetians* had flower forms coming out of them. 1 9 9 9

The list goes on and on about the wonders of the material that is glass. It has incredible strength. It's the only material you can really blow. Its raw materials are common and cheap. It's made up of, really, sand. You take sand and fire and put it together, and you can have glass. And it turns into a liquid. Imagine, the sand turns into a liquid! 1 9 9 6

What I really like to do is have people make things without thinking about how they're designed. The hardest part for me to work with other artists is to get them to work

in a way where they're not "designers," or they're not "artists." I don't like my work to look as if it's been put together by someone who has a label. I like it to look as if it were put together by nature. And so the quicker you put glass up, and the less you think about it, very often the better the piece looks. 1 9 9 8

Since 1975, I've done about eight or nine series. Each started in a different way: some evolved from one series, others started abruptly, and still others began out of frustration. . . . This raises the question, "How far do you experiment with an idea?" Then at what point do you decide, "I'm going to really pursue this." And at what point do you decide, "Not only am I going to pursue it, I am going to exhibit it." It is a question of taking chances. 1 9 9 0

My strongest memories from the European cathedrals were the windows. And I think that would probably be true for many people. It's not just because I had a big fascination for glass. I mean, how do you walk into a cathedral with that rose window there and not just love it? 1 9 9 8

Then, along comes somebody and figures out that you can gather it up on the end of a blowpipe, blow into it, human breath, and make a bubble. Imagine the thought. Who would've thought of this? Was it an accident? 1 9 9 7

Isn't it unbelievable that the most fragile of materials, glass, is also the most permanent material? 1 9 9 3

I know if I go down to the glass shop right now and work down there, I'm going to make something that has never

been made before. That in itself is an inspiration, the fact that I can go down and make something that no one's ever seen before, even though they've been making stuff out of glass for five thousand years. I don't know why that's easy for me to do, but it is. 1 9 9 8

I don't like things "designed." I like them when they look like they just happened to be like that. The more the better! 1 9 9 7

From the very beginning, when I began with glass (almost within the first few weeks of my working with it), I was involved with organic aspects of the liquidity . . . the natural sort of watery, fluid qualities of the material. If you go back to my early installations, I started blowing glass in '66, and already by '67, wherever I could find places I'd take a glob of molten glass, climb up on a

ladder and let it drip down and form shapes, and blow in it at the same time. Sometimes I'd make little molds that it would go into. 1994

A lot of creativity has to do with energy, confidence, and focus. These are the elements for making creative things. It's probably the same thing in whether you're making a movie, whether you're an entrepreneur doing a business, whether you're an artist, or whether you're a gardener or a cook. These are all the same qualities that it takes. 1994

I don't use a lot of molds or a lot of tools, so it has a natural feel. I use centrifugal force and gravity and fire. I use those elements to shape the glass. 2000

I went to the doctor yesterday, and while I was in the pharmacy getting a prescription, a ninety-three-year-old

lady came up to me and told me how great it was to see a show of mine a couple of years ago. And I can't tell you what a thrill it was to stand there and talk, and to see the joy on her face, sharing with me the artwork that had brought something to her life. 1 9 9 8

Jack Lenor Larson recommended I teach at Haystack in 1967. I had an extraordinary life-changing experience there and was so overwhelmed by everything—the architecture, the site, the people, the social structure, and, more than anything, Fran Merritt. I taught four years in a row and really got to know Fran and Priscilla. I idolized Fran and wanted to be just like him. I started to think about a glass center that would be patterned after Haystack. In 1971, the Pilchuck Glass School did get started on the opposite coast and to this day is very similar in size and structure to Haystack. Pilchuck

would not exist if it weren't for Haystack and Fran and Priscilla Merritt. 2 0 0 1

As you write a letter, of course, you're thinking. It's simply a way to make your mind work. Nothing works better than writing a letter, if you have an idea. 1 9 9 8

I don't think much about the past. I think more about the future. I prefer to be thinking about what I want to be doing tomorrow.

In the summer of 1977, I was visiting the Tacoma Historical Society with Italo Scanga. I was struck by a pile of Northwest Coast Indian baskets that were stacked one inside another. They were dented and misshapen, wonderful forms. I don't really know what made me want to reproduce them. 1 9 8 6

I think of something, I go immediately to voice mail and leave a message. It's one thing to think about something. It's one thing to have an idea. It's another thing to do it. That really separates the doer from the thinker. You have to have both. You have to be able to do it. Many things require action immediately. 1 9 9 8

The drawings on the cylinders are very spontaneous and molten. They relied on chance and gravity, like the work that followed it, and the work that preceded it. . . . The drawings are very much as I like to work, which is quick and immediate and spontaneous, with an element of change, with a mystery about it. 1 9 8 6

Why glass? Suppose a child comes upon some beach glass with sun on it. The little kid will drop everything to get that. Maybe I'm that little kid. 1 9 9 6

Because I don't blow glass anymore, maybe I get a little frustrated, and it's not very hands-on for me, so I'll be making drawings outside on the deck, and the drawings really help me think about things. I work with a lot of color, and that inspires me and maybe it inspires them, to see me back there working on ideas. And I rely very heavily on them to look at the drawings, and the gaffers to see things in the drawings. 2 0 0 1

I started making up a color chart with one color for the interior, another color for the exterior, and a contrasting color for the lip wrap, along with various jimmies and dusts of pigment between the gathers of glass. Throughout the blowing process, colors were added, layer upon layer. Each piece was another experiment. When we unloaded the ovens in the morning, there was a rush of seeing something never seen before. Like much

of my work, the series inspired itself. The unbelievable combinations of color—that was the driving force. 1993

I thought it was the hot glass that was so mysterious, but then I realized it was the air that went into it that was miraculous. 1997

In glassblowing, the faster you learn to make a form, the more natural it seems. I want my work to appear like it came from nature—so that if someone found it on a beach or in the forest, they might think it belonged there. 1996

I feel very fortunate to be able to have such talent working with me, especially now that I am getting more involved with large architectural projects and installations. I suppose it would be possible to do these things on one's own, but the whole process would just be too slow for me.

Glassblowing is a very spontaneous and fast medium. You have to respond very quickly. I like working fast, and the team allows me to do that. 1 9 9 2

Some [pieces] will be made out of Polyvitro, a type of polymer that's actually plastic, because the finished forms look different than glass, they're lighter, and you can hang them from certain things you couldn't hang glass from. 2 0 0 1

Two years ago I went with my team to a little island in Tokyo Bay far offshore. . . . We were invited over to go blow glass for two weeks and demonstrate for the students. When I did an installation of the *Floats* at the American Craft Museum, I called it *Niijima Floats* in honor of the little island with the beautiful glass shop. 1 9 9 2

When we arrived we started blowing right away and then for seven days straight. . . . We made about 2,000 pieces of glass and hung the *Chandeliers* around the village. There was only about three hours' darkness at night so we worked nearly all the time. A lot of the villagers got involved, and we ended up carrying the glass all over the place. We'd hang it from a bridge, then toss it in the river so that it could float downstream, and then the villagers would gather it with their rowboats and hand it up to our team so they could hang it in a tree or something. They'd never seen anything like it before—it was wild! 1 9 9 6

At the time I came to Venice, all the glass artists in the States worked by themselves. When I came over here I realized that if you worked with half a dozen or more people you could achieve things you could never do alone. Back at home, I started working with my RISD students

as a team. And from that point on, I've worked with a team. 1996

The role models for young people today are athletes, movie stars, rock-and-roll singers, and that's kind of a sad state of affairs. I like the idea that I can get young people interested in something they can do themselves. 1977

I was born in Tacoma, Washington, an industrial town south of Seattle. Neither one of my parents went to college. My dad was in the coal mines up on Mount Rainier with the rest of his brothers. He was the only one to sort of get out of the mines and get a job in town, initially, I think, as a butcher, and then eventually became a union organizer for the AFL-CIO. 1998

I don't know what it is about glass and me. It's just my material—it's the one I like to work with. There's nothing like it. I mean, plastic looks like glass, I suppose, but it isn't. "Plastic has no history," my good friend Italo Scanga once said, but glass does. Glass has been there forever. It's in the earth; it's made up of sand.

It's tough because I fail a lot. I question my own aesthetics much of the time. I'll make something and really like it, and then a couple months later not like it. I don't know. 1974

Somebody once said that people become artists because they have a certain kind of energy to release, and that rang true to me. It's not the kind of energy you can work off in the weight room. That's really why I draw. 1992

The water is really important to me. Like I love to be on the ocean, I love baths, I love showers, I love swimming. I think a lot when I'm in the water. 1 9 9 9

I never gave assignments as a teacher; I didn't believe in them. And I believed that you had to be self-motivated, and I felt the way to remain motivated was to work from and off the other students, myself, and the visiting artists that I would bring into the department. I also insisted that all work be photographed, so I rarely looked at actual work. Reviews were given from slides. Twice a semester, we would meet in a room, very often a conference center in a hotel, banquet room, or something. All day long, slides were shown of the student's projects. By the time people that worked with me had gone through the Rhode Island School of Design, their work was fully documented, and they were able to talk about their work.

They usually developed a personal style of their own. 1998

One night I melted a few pounds of stained glass in one of my kilns and dipped a steel pipe from the basement into it. I blew into the pipe and a bubble of glass appeared. I had never seen glassblowing before. My fascination for it probably comes in part from discovering the process that night by accident. From that moment, I became obsessed with learning all I could about glass. 1986

My series *Niijima Floats* are the first pieces I have made that I feel could go outside. Because the hole in the piece faces down, there's no place for water to collect and freeze, which is normally a problem for exterior pieces. 1992

You know, you don't teach art. . . . That's the last thing you'd ever teach, is how to make art. All you have to do is set up the environment and it happens. 1998

The *Baskets* went on to inform many of the series that followed. The *Seaforms, Macchia,* and *Soft Cylinders* all came directly from the style of blowing that I had developed for the *Baskets*. This blowing technique was the result of my trying to make the forms appear as natural as possible. This meant letting glass find its own form.

What is it about the light in Jerusalem that makes it the City of Light? You can't explain exactly what is. It's a feeling. It's a look. But it has it. There is this beautiful, golden light that bathes Jerusalem. 1999

When I do works in public spaces . . . I want to make the most creative thing I can. And the freshest thing that I can. Importantly, I want the public to be able to respond to the piece. Obviously, you can't please all the people all the time, but I would like to think that what I've created here does something to a lot of people from a lot of different backgrounds. 2 0 0 1

"What did I learn from this thing?" "What happened?" "What the hell was I doing?" I'm sure everybody questions what I did. 1 9 9 4

And so when you're working with transparent materials, when you're looking at glass, plastic, ice, or water, you're looking at light itself. The light is coming through, and you see that cobalt blue, that ruby red, whatever the color might be—you're looking at the light and the color

mix together. Something magical and mystical, something we don't understand, nor should we care to understand. Sort of like trying to understand the moon. Water has magical powers, and glass has magical powers. So does plastic, and so does ice. 1 9 9 9

Glass, ice—I love ice—plastics, these are all materials that are all different but that are all transparent, very luminous, and color can go through in such incredible ways.

So you take sand, and fire, and put them together and you have glass. Imagine! The sand turns into a liquid, and you stick a pipe down there and gather it up like honey and bring it out and blow down the pipe, and you get a bubble that over the centuries glassblowers have learned to make into an incredible array of shapes. And

I've been lucky enough to come along at the right time and the right place to be able to expand many of the forms that were made over this 2,000-year history. 1 9 9 8

Artists have to be completely unafraid to do what ideas that they have. They have to push the envelope. They must not be afraid to do what comes to them. And that's why there are probably so many cases of artists that led strange lives. You can't get there without going to where your passion takes you. 2 0 0 0

The whole idea of making art, as far as I'm concerned, comes from doing it over and over and over again. You must make a lot of mistakes. A problem these days is that students are becoming afraid to fail—I have eighteen- or nineteen-year-old students who are concerned if this piece is going to be a failure or not. They'll go home and

they'll worry about it for a couple of weeks, get it all sorted out in their minds—I'm really against that attitude of working. 1 9 7 4

I think ideas come a great deal from being alone. Even though I work with a big team of people all day long, I happen to be an early riser, so I'm often up at four or five in the morning and have several hours to be on my own to think about things. 1 9 9 9

Important ideas come from some flash in the pan—some moment—and something that you can't describe. 1 9 8 8

The only explanation I'm ever able to give about where things come from is "energy." That has to come out in one way or another. Sometimes it's more destructive, sometimes it's more beautiful, sometimes more creative.

Energy can go in so many directions, and you have to harness it. Correction! You don't harness it, you use it. You put it to good use. 1 9 9 6

Working—just working with glass, working outside, which I used to do and still like to do. Even just simple sheets of stained glass that I bought and then put up in different configurations. 1 9 9 9

I'm drawing, you know, fifty pencils in each hand. And I draw over glass or over rice or beans. My mother used to watch me draw, and she'd just shake her head and walk away wondering what the hell I was doing. 1 9 9 8

I never got completely absorbed into the blowing process. Even though my work comes out of the miraculous process of glassblowing, and often develops from it, my

real love was never the glassblowing, but the object itself. And really I've always been interested in space. Even when I made the *Cylinders*, the single object cylinders, or the *Macchia*, my interest remained in space. I was thinking not of the object but how the object would look in a room. 1998

Yeah, it's hard work, it's physical hard work, and it helps to be athletic. But mostly you have to be motivated. Glass is so spontaneous, so immediate, that it inspires almost anyone to work with it, the sense of accomplishment, and the danger, and the excitement. It's all one package. 2000

I'm not the type of artist whose work evolved over a logical progression. It's not the way I work. I work on some series that you might say evolves, but then there will be something very fresh and new that appears which

didn't make any sense. I like that. I like to be motivated by new things. If I had to do the same thing all the time, I would get bored out of my mind. 1997

Anybody that knows me realizes that I like to work fast, and that the faster it is, the more energy it takes, and the better I like it. I know the work is gonna turn out better if it's done quickly. If I try to rework things, they never come out as good. 2002

I'm always looking forward to opening the ovens in the morning. 1995

It's exciting to make something you've never made before. That's what we try to do. But that's a difficult challenge. I know that if I don't do something new I'm not going to be happy. And so you look, you try to find something.

Things go wrong, all of a sudden nobody's making anything interesting. But then you get lucky and something starts to happen. 1996

The thing is that I never really intended for my studio to get this big. On the other hand, I let it get this big. And maybe I let it get this big because it allows me to have the freedom to do what I want to do. You often have to have freedom.

Obviously, it wasn't a conscious decision to work with glass. It started, I'm sure, back when I was a little kid, walking on the beach somewhere, I found a little bit of glass. It may have been a bottle . . . broken on a rock into a hundred pieces, which was then dispersed on the beach for a hundred different kids to find.

While the team is working, I can walk over to the drawing board and begin to draw. Being able to move back and forth between the pad and the drawing table is what really allowed the series to move so quickly. . . . Drawing is a fluid process for me, like glassblowing is a movement of liquid.

Lino [Tagliapietra] had been coming to Pilchuck for years, but I had never worked with European masters, because my work had always been unorthodox and asymmetrical, and the idea of working with a European master didn't make sense. But Lino and I decided that we'd try to do something together, so I designed a series that was a takeoff from some Venetian Art Deco pieces I had seen that were from the 1920s. And I was able to sketch them, and from those sketches, Lino began to work on the Venetians.

Unlike a lot of people that make things, I get more enjoyment from seeing the final product, the actual exhibition, because that's where the work really shines. Thousands of people will get to see it and hopefully derive much joy from it. 2 0 0 1

Who knows what's next? You know, when people say, "What are you gonna do next?" I always say if I knew what I was going to do next, I'd be doing it.

We see what it's like when people come in and how they feel and what joy the glass brings them, not everybody, but a lot of people. I think a majority of the people enjoy my work and lot of other artists' work. I think it brings something to our culture that we desperately need.

Thanks Everybody

love

Chuck

9·17·02

April Adams	Martin Blank	Anna Katherine Curfman
Laura Aguiar	Carol Bobanick	Keegan Curnutt
Kirsten Akre	Lars Borgeson	Jamie Daniels
Hector Alers	Jocelyn Boyea	Joey de Camp
Angelynne Amores	Tucker Brandt	Thea De Francesco
Ginger Anderson	Roger Bransteitter	Dex Decker
Parks Anderson	Michael Bray	Sam Decker
Rahman Anderson	Mark Bridgwood	Nadège Desgenétz
Lisa Arizzi	Eugene Broadgate	Paul DeSomma
Damon Arndt	Jenny Brown	David Doig
Paul Arnhold	Susan Brown	Ken Dolan
Dustin Ashlock	Diane Caillier	Oliver Doriss
Andre Asselin	Jeremy Canwell	Evagelos Drinis
Eric Augino	Scott Carlson	Leonard Duboff
William Barnes	Natasha Carnell	Randy DuRussel
Drew Becher	Domonic Ceccarelli	Mary Dykkesten
Levi Belber	Shaun Chappell	Alex Earle
Jeffrey Bender	Kristin Chasteen	Curt Eckman
John Bennett	Nils Christian	Grant Eckman
Joe Benvenuto	Steven Cillian	Lydia Eckman
Ed Berg	Sylvia Cisneros	Kate Elliott
Danny Berger	Ken Clark	Lise Ellner
Kai-Uwe Bergmann	Jan Cook	Romi Epstein
Bruce Bertalmio	Jack Crane	Tillman Erb
Megan Bingham	Jonas Criscoe	Michael Fielding
Marsha Blaker-DeSomma	Jacque Culver	Tom Fobes
Chris Blanchard	Paul Cunningham	Michael Fox

Fritz Frauchiger

Dan Friday

Daisy Fry

David Gackenbach

Bonnie Gallagher

Jeff Gerber

Manisone Gipson

Dorothy Giriat

Catherine Gray

Heather Gray

Thomas Gray

Carson Grieve

Carl Grimm

Anita Gross

Leanne Hart

Gary Hayden

Janice Hebert

Michael Holberg

Derek Hollinsworth

Brook Hovorka

Eric Huebsch

Lisa Huston

Etsuko Ichikawa

Lori Isley

Bryan Jablonski

Leslie Jackson

Calder Jacobs

Paula Jacobson

Diana Johnson

Karin Johnson

Nickalene Johnson

Douglas Jordan

Erin Kantola

John Karabats

Wilbur Kelly

Lara Khoury

Karin Kidder

Mary Kilimann

Robin Kimmerling

Brian Koontz

Jordan Kube

Peter Kuhnlein

John Landon

Joel Langholz

Mike Lash

Lisa Leach

Ruth Lednicer

Scott Leen

Nathan Lesnett

Elissa Levine

Jennifer Lewis

Tom Lind

Bobby Lloyd

Ashley Long

John Lucchesini

Lisa MacDonald

Laurence Madrelle

Anthony Maglalang

Janet Makela

Dante Marioni

Duane Marsh

Daniel McCraw

Ed McDonald

Mark McDonnell

Katherine McGuire

Thomas McHugh

Bennett McKnight

Erin McNamara

Michael Meeker

Robbie Miller

Zane Mills

James Milostan

Michael Moeller

Paula Mohs

Joan Monetta

Jim Mongrain

Ben Moore

Rachel Moore

Jason Mouer

Beverly Mundy

Karen Mutch

Britt Nelson	Rich Royal	Boyd Sugiki
Michael Nelson	Julianna Ross Royer	Joshua Swanson
Bonnie Niccum	Bryan Rubino	Yvonne Swanson
Nancy Nilsen	Mark Rubino	Kelly Tallariti
Billy O'Neill	Eunita Rushing	Chris Tedesco
Masako Onodera	Kim Ryan	Denise Thomas
Dennis Palin	Tracy Savage	Kiert Thomforde
DJ Palin	Nadine Saylor	Catherine Thorbeck
Debbie Parmenter	Lisa Schamp-Bieles	Kristin Trent
Byron Parnell	Ollie Schubert	Allen Vinup
Charlie Parriott	Adam Schwerner	Greg Vriethoff
Eric Pauli	Angela Scott	Paul Wallace
Wynne Pei	Ali Shahvali	Dave Walters
Marie Pellaton	Gary Shaleen	Terry Waugh
Erik Phillips	Greg Sharp	Chad Wentzel
Rebecca Pool	Rachel Shumate	Peter West
Jeff Price	Joanna Sikes	Mike White
Todd Priebe	Soren Sinclair	Paula Wolf Dillon
Bo Ramos	Preston Singletary	Molly Wolfe
Josh Raskob	Richard Slovak	Eric Woll
Annette Ringe	Daryl Smith	Suzanne Wood
Teresa Rishel	Megan Smith	Patsy Wootten
Terry Rishel	Ryan Smith	Lauren Wozny
Lisa Roberts	Sadie Smith	Chantal Younis
Paddy Rolleston	Julie Staton	
Barry Rosen	Laurel Stephenson	
Ashley Rowley	Alex Stisser	

Museum Collections

Akita Senshu Museum of Art, Akita, Japan

Akron Art Museum, Akron, Ohio

Albany Museum of Art, Albany, Georgia

Albright-Knox Art Gallery, Buffalo, New York

Allied Arts Association, Richland, Washington

American Craft Museum, New York, New York

Amon Carter Museum, Fort Worth, Texas

Anchorage Museum of History and Art, Anchorage, Alaska

Arizona State University Art Museum, Tempe, Arizona

Arkansas Arts Center, Little Rock, Arkansas

Art Gallery of Greater Victoria, Victoria, British Columbia, Canada

Art Gallery of Western Australia, Perth, Australia

Art Museum of Missoula, Missoula, Montana

Art Museum of Southeast Texas, Beaumont, Texas

Asheville Art Museum, Asheville, North Carolina

Auckland Museum, Auckland, New Zealand

Azabu Museum of Arts and Crafts, Tokyo, Japan

Ball State University Museum of Art, Muncie, Indiana

Beach Museum of Art, Kansas State University, Manhattan, Kansas

Bellevue Art Museum, Bellevue, Washington

Berkeley Art Museum, University of California, Berkeley, California

Birmingham Museum of Art, Birmingham, Alabama

Boarman Arts Center, Martinsburg, West Virginia

Boca Raton Museum of Art, Boca Raton, Florida

Brooklyn Museum, Brooklyn, New York

Canadian Clay & Glass Gallery, Waterloo, Ontario, Canada

Canadian Craft Museum, Vancouver, British Columbia, Canada

Carnegie Museum of Art, Pittsburgh, Pennsylvania

Charles A. Wustum Museum of Fine Arts, Racine, Wisconsin

Chrysler Museum of Art, Norfolk, Virginia

Cincinnati Art Museum, Cincinnati, Ohio

Cleveland Center for Contemporary Art, Cleveland, Ohio

Cleveland Museum of Art, Cleveland, Ohio

Columbus Cultural Arts Center, Columbus, Ohio

Columbus Museum of Art, Columbus, Ohio

Contemporary Arts Center, Cincinnati, Ohio

Contemporary Crafts Association and Gallery, Portland, OR

Contemporary Museum, Honolulu, Hawaii

Cooper-Hewitt, National Design Museum, Smithsonian Institution,

New York, New York

Corcoran Gallery of Art, Washington, D.C.

Corning Museum of Glass, Corning, New York

Crocker Art Museum, Sacramento, California

Currier Gallery of Art, Manchester, New Hampshire

Daiichi Museum, Nagoya, Japan

Dallas Museum of Art, Dallas, Texas

Danske Kunstindustrimuseum, Copenhagen, Denmark

David Winton Bell Gallery, Brown University, Providence, Rhode Island

Dayton Art Institute, Dayton, Ohio

DeCordova Museum and Sculpture Park, Lincoln, Massachusetts

Delaware Art Museum, Wilmington, Delaware

Denver Art Museum, Denver, Colorado

Detroit Institute of Arts, Detroit, Michigan

Dowse Art Museum, Lower Hutt, New Zealand

Elvehjem Museum of Art, University of Wisconsin, Madison, Wisconsin

Eretz Israel Museum, Tel Aviv, Israel

Everson Museum of Art, Syracuse, New York

Experience Music Project, Seattle, Washington

Fine Arts Institute, Edmond, Oklahoma

Flint Institute of Arts, Flint, Michigan

Galéria mesta Bratislavy, Bratislava, Slovakia

Glasmuseum, Ebeltoft, Denmark

Glasmuseum, Frauenau, Germany

Glasmuseum alter Hof Herding, Glascollection, Ernsting, Germany

Glasmuseum Wertheim, Wertheim, Germany

Grand Rapids Art Museum, Grand Rapids, Michigan

Hakone Glass Forest, Ukai Museum, Hakone, Japan

Hawke's Bay Exhibition Centre, Hastings, New Zealand

High Museum of Art, Atlanta, Georgia

Hiroshima City Museum of Contemporary Art, Hiroshima, Japan

Hokkaido Museum of Modern Art, Hokkaido, Japan

Honolulu Academy of Arts, Honolulu, Hawaii

Hunter Museum of American Art, Chattanooga, Tennessee

Indianapolis Museum of Art, Indianapolis, Indiana

Israel Museum, Jerusalem, Israel

Japan Institute of Arts and Crafts, Tokyo, Japan

Jesse Besser Museum, Alpena, Michigan

Jesuit Dallas Museum, Dallas, Texas

Joslyn Art Museum, Omaha, Nebraska

Jundt Art Museum, Gonzaga University, Spokane, Washington

Kalamazoo Institute of Arts, Kalamazoo, Michigan

Kaohsiung Museum of Fine Arts, Kaohsiung, Taiwan

Kemper Museum of Contemporary Art, Kansas City, Missouri

Kestner-Gesellschaft, Hannover, Germany

Kobe City Museum, Kobe, Japan

Krannert Art Museum, University of Illinois, Champaign, Illinois

Krasl Art Center, St. Joseph, Michigan

Kunstmuseum Düsseldorf, Düsseldorf, Germany

Kunstsammlungen der Veste Coburg, Coburg, Germany

Kurita Museum, Tochigi, Japan

Leigh Yawkey Woodson Art Museum, Wausau, Wisconsin

Lobmeyr Museum, Vienna, Austria

LongHouse Reserve, East Hampton, New York

Los Angeles County Museum of Art, Los Angeles, California

Lowe Art Museum, University of Miami, Coral Gables, Florida

Lyman Allyn Art Museum, New London, Connecticut

M.H. de Young Memorial Museum, San Francisco, California

Madison Art Center, Madison, Wisconsin

Manawatu Museum, Palmerston North, New Zealand

Matsushita Art Museum, Kagoshima, Japan

Meguro Museum of Art, Tokyo, Japan

Memorial Art Gallery, University of Rochester, Rochester, New York

Metropolitan Museum of Art, New York, New York

Milwaukee Art Museum, Milwaukee, Wisconsin

Minneapolis Institute of Arts, Minneapolis, Minnesota

Mint Museum of Craft + Design, Charlotte, North Carolina

Mobile Museum of Art, Mobile, Alabama

Modern Art Museum of Fort Worth, Fort Worth, Texas

Montreal Museum of Fine Arts, Montreal, Quebec, Canada

Morris Museum, Morristown, New Jersey

Musée d'Art Moderne et d'Art Contemporain, Nice, France

Musée des Arts Décoratifs, Lausanne, Switzerland

Musée des Arts Décoratifs, Palais du Louvre, Paris, France

Musée des Beaux-Arts et de la Céramique, Rouen, France

Musée Provincial Sterckshof, Antwerp, Belgium

Museo del Vidrio, Monterrey, Mexico

Museum Bellerive, Zurich, Switzerland

Museum Boijmans Van Beuningen, Rotterdam, The Netherlands

Museum für Kunst und Gewerbe Hamburg, Hamburg, Germany

Museum für Kunsthandwerk, Frankfurt am Main, Germany

Museum of American Glass at Wheaton Village, Millville, New Jersey

Museum of Art, Rhode Island School of Design, Providence, Rhode Island

Museum of Art and Archaeology, Columbia, Missouri

Museum of Art Fort Lauderdale, Fort Lauderdale, Florida

Museum of Arts and Sciences, Daytona Beach, Florida

Museum of Contemporary Art, Chicago, Illinois

Museum of Contemporary Art at San Diego, La Jolla, California

Museum of Fine Arts, Boston, Massachusetts

Museum of Fine Arts, Houston, Houston, Texas

Museum of Fine Arts, St. Petersburg, Florida

Museum of Modern Art, New York, New York

Museum of Northwest Art, La Conner, Washington

Museum voor Sierkunst en Vormgeving, Ghent, Belgium

Muskegon Museum of Art, Muskegon, Michigan

Muzeum města Brna, Brno, Czech Republic

Muzeum skla a bižuterie, Jablonec nad Nisou, Czech Republic

Múzeum židovskej kultúry, Bratislava, Slovakia

Naples Museum of Art, Naples, Florida

National Gallery of Australia, Canberra, Australia

National Gallery of Victoria, Melbourne, Australia

National Liberty Museum, Philadelphia, Pennsylvania

National Museum Kyoto, Kyoto, Japan

National Museum of American History, Smithsonian Institution, Washington, D.C.

National Museum of Modern Art Kyoto, Kyoto, Japan

National Museum of Modern Art Tokyo, Tokyo, Japan

Nationalmuseum, Stockholm, Sweden

New Orleans Museum of Art, New Orleans, Louisiana

Newport Harbor Art Museum, Newport Beach, California

Niijima Contemporary Art Museum, Niijima, Japan

North Central Washington Museum, Wenatchee, Washington

Notojima Glass Art Museum, Ishikawa, Japan

O Art Museum, Tokyo, Japan

Oklahoma City Museum of Art, Oklahoma City, Oklahoma

Otago Museum, Dunedin, New Zealand

Palm Beach Community College Museum of Art, Lake Worth, Florida

Palm Springs Desert Museum, Palm Springs, California

Palmer Museum of Art, Pennsylvania State University, University Park, Pennsylvania

Parrish Art Museum, Southampton, New York

Philadelphia Museum of Art, Philadelphia, Pennsylvania

Phoenix Art Museum, Phoenix, Arizona

Plains Art Museum, Fargo, North Dakota

Portland Art Museum, Portland, Oregon

Portland Museum of Art, Portland, Maine

Powerhouse Museum, Sydney, Australia

Princeton University Art Museum, Princeton, New Jersey

Queensland Art Gallery, South Brisbane, Australia

Robert McDougall Art Gallery, Christchurch, New Zealand

Royal Ontario Museum, Toronto, Ontario, Canada

Saint Louis Art Museum, St. Louis, Missouri

Samuel P. Harn Museum of Art, University of Florida, Gainesville, Florida

San Francisco Museum of Modern Art, San Francisco, California

San Jose Museum of Art, San Jose, California

Scitech Discovery Centre, Perth, Australia

Scottsdale Center for the Arts, Scottsdale, Arizona

Seattle Art Museum, Seattle, Washington

Shimonoseki City Art Museum, Shimonoseki, Japan

Singapore Art Museum, Singapore

Slovenská národná galéria, Bratislava, Slovakia

Smith College Museum of Art, Northampton, Massachusetts

Smithsonian American Art Museum, Washington, D.C.

Sogetsu Art Museum, Tokyo, Japan

Speed Art Museum, Louisville, Kentucky

Spencer Museum of Art, University of Kansas, Lawrence, Kansas

Springfield Museum of Fine Arts, Springfield, Massachusetts

Štátna galéria Banská Bystrica, Banská Bystrica, Slovakia

Suntory Museum of Art, Tokyo, Japan

Suomen Lasimuseo, Riihimäki, Finland

Suwa Garasu no Sato Museum, Nagano, Japan

Tacoma Art Museum, Tacoma, Washington

Taipei Fine Arts Museum, Taipei, Taiwan

Tochigi Prefectural Museum of Fine Arts, Tochigi, Japan

Toledo Museum of Art, Toledo, Ohio

Uměleckoprůmsylové muzeum, Prague, Czech Republic

Utah Museum of Fine Arts, University of Utah, Salt Lake City, Utah

Victoria and Albert Museum, London, England

Wadsworth Atheneum, Hartford, Connecticut

Waikato Museum of Art and History, Hamilton, New Zealand

Walker Hill Art Center, Seoul, South Korea

Whatcom Museum of History and Art, Bellingham, Washington

White House Collection of American Crafts, Washington, D.C.

Whitney Museum of American Art, New York, New York

Württembergisches Landesmuseum Stuttgart, Stuttgart, Germany

Yale University Art Gallery, New Haven, Connecticut

Yokohama Museum of Art, Yokohama, Japan

This fifth printing of Chihuly Gardens & Glass
is limited to 5.000 casebound copies.
The entire contents are copyright © 2002 Dale Chihuly.
All rights reserved. Quotes by Dale Chihuly.

Every effort has been made to determine that the historical postcards
included in this book are of an age that places them in the public domain.

Photographs
Shaun Chappell. Jan Cook. Robin Coomer. Paul Fisher. Claire Garoutte.
Jeff Gerber. Itamar Grinberg. Russell Johnson. Ansgard Kaliss.
Scott M. Leen. Teresa N. Rishel. Terry Rishel. Karola Ritter. Rik Sferra

Design Team
Natasha Carnell. Anna Katherine Curfman.
Laurence Madrelle. Jeff Price. Barry Rosen

Typeface Bauer Bodoni
Paper White A matt art 157 gsm

Printing and binding
Hing Yip Printing Co.. Ltd.. China

Portland Press
PO Box 70856. Seattle. Washington 98127
800 574 7272
www.portlandpress.net
ISBN 1-57684-018-2